planet earth
our extraordinary world

Cool Creatures

Modern Publishing
A Division of Unisystems, Inc.
New York, New York 10022
Printed in the U.S.A.
Series UPC: 49060

Wild Dog

Flamingos like to stand on one leg.

Iguana

Penguin and Seal

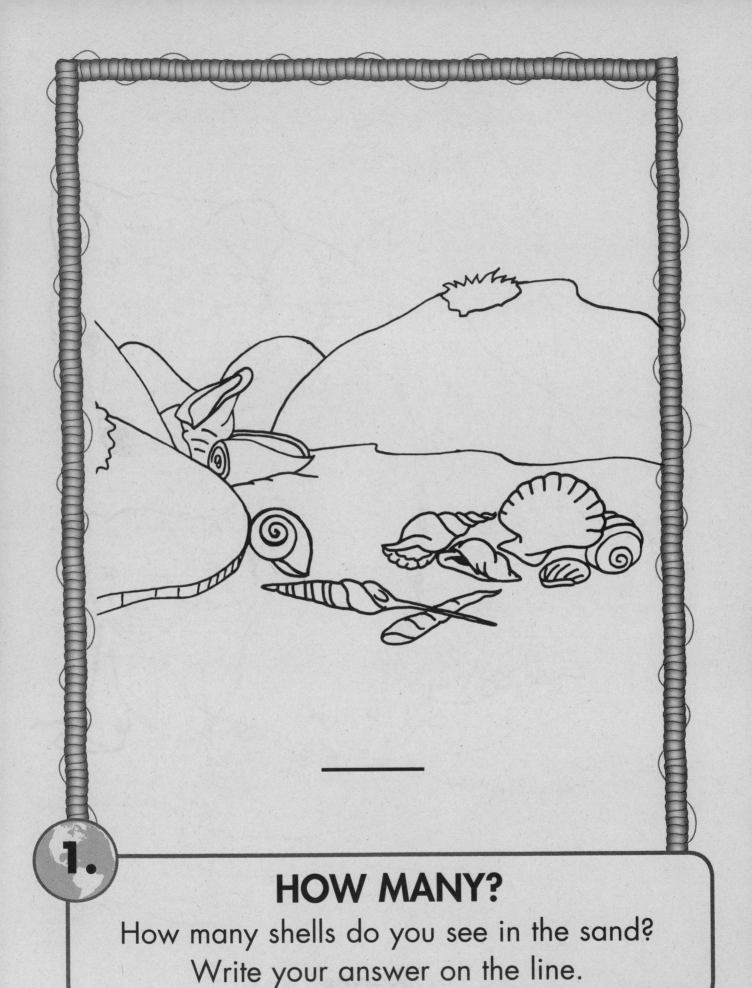

1.

HOW MANY?

How many shells do you see in the sand?
Write your answer on the line.

See Answers

Bears

Jaguar

Sea Otters

Llama

A panda can eat up to 88 pounds of bamboo a day!

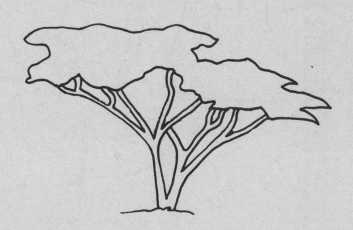

Plains

2.

NUMBER FINDER

Can you find the numbers 1-9 in this beautiful waterfall? Color them!

Bats

Octopus

Tortoise

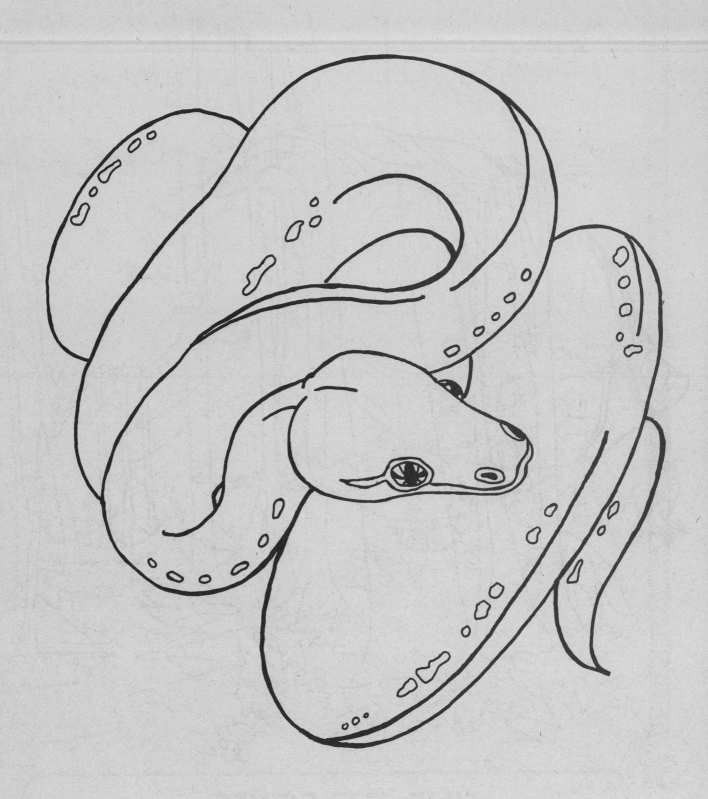

Anaconda

3.

FIND THE FOXES
Can you spot the 5 hidden foxes in this forest?
Circle them!

See Answers

Aardvarks are found on the African plains and feed mainly on termites.

Polar Bear

Dolphin

Wolf

Fish

Tortoise

Bobcat

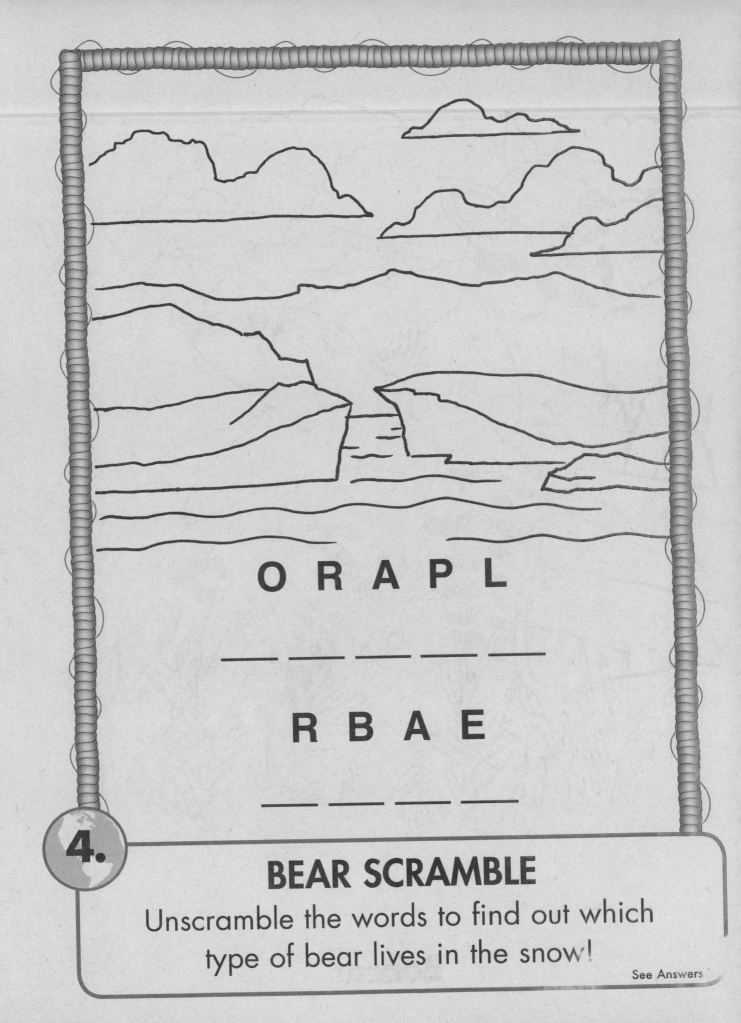

O R A P L

— — — — —

R B A E

— — — —

4.

BEAR SCRAMBLE
Unscramble the words to find out which
type of bear lives in the snow!

See Answers

Shark

Elephants

1.

2.

3.

4.

5.

COUNTING CAMELS
Camels use their humps for storing water.
Which group of camels has the most humps?
Circle them!

See Answers

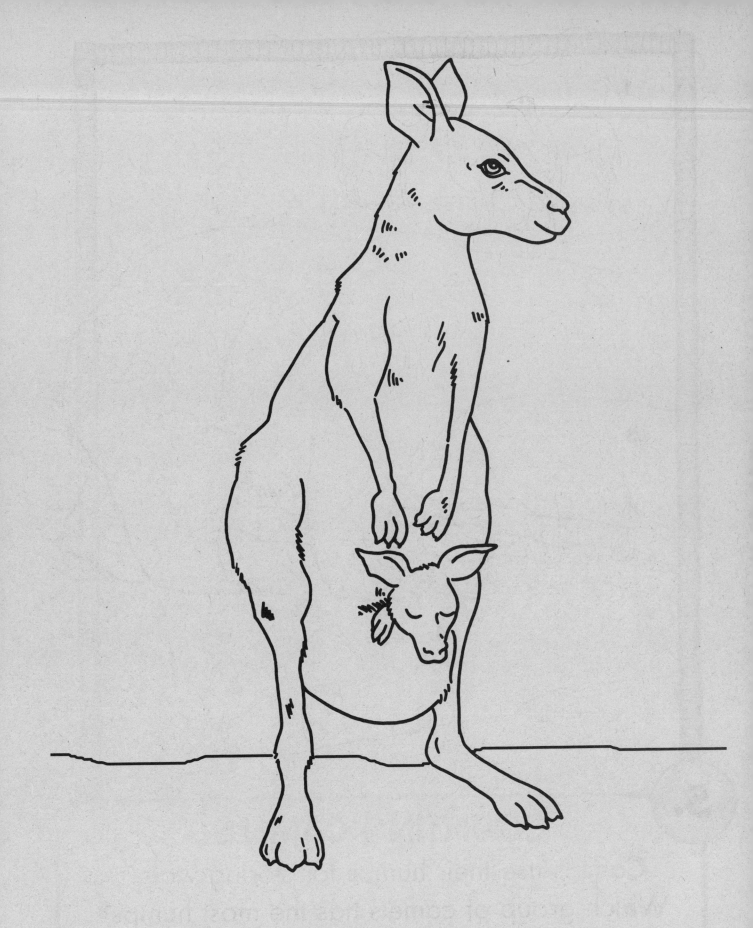

Kangaroo

Polar bears weigh up to 1,260 pounds.

Kangaroo Rat

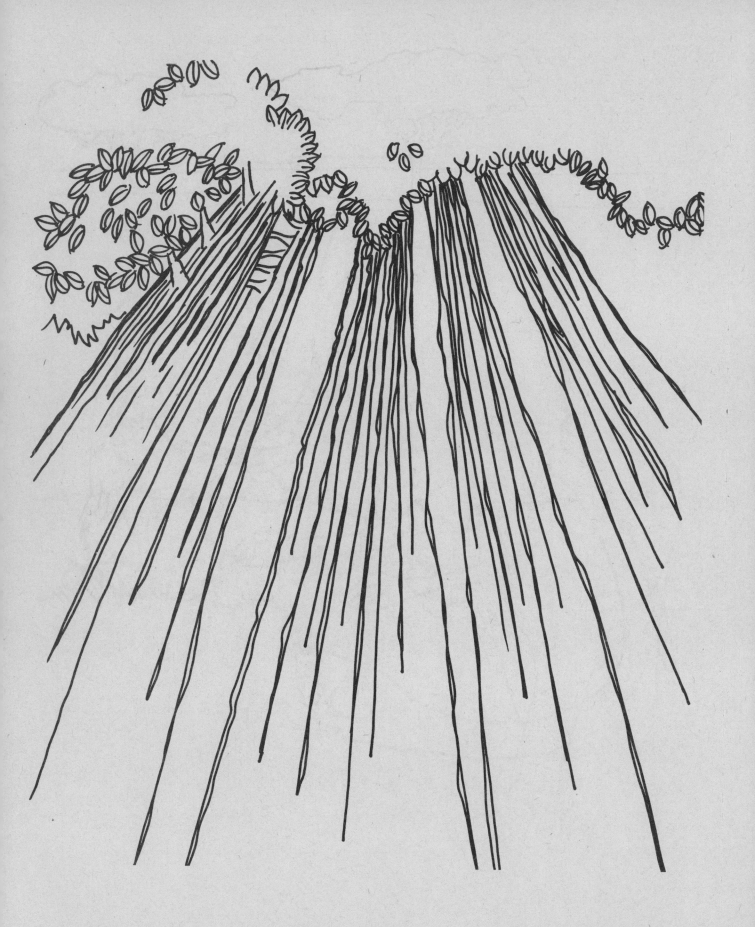

Redwoods are the tallest known trees!

Lions

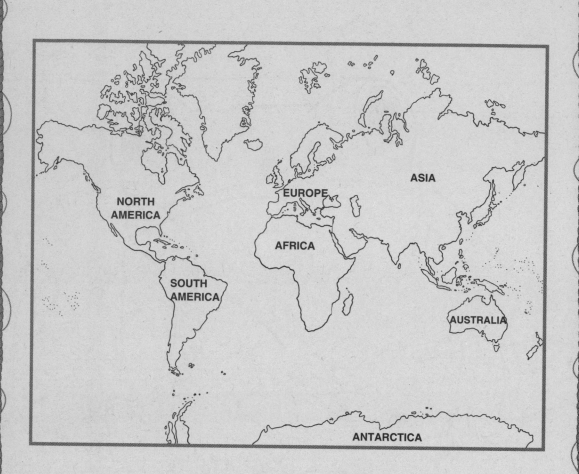

NORTH AMERICA

EUROPE

ASIA

AFRICA

SOUTH AMERICA

AUSTRALIA

ANTARCTICA

_____

6.

THE LETTER A

How many times do you see the letter A appear in all 7 continents?
Write your answer on the line!

See Answers

**Flying frogs live in trees
in tropical forests.**

Tiger

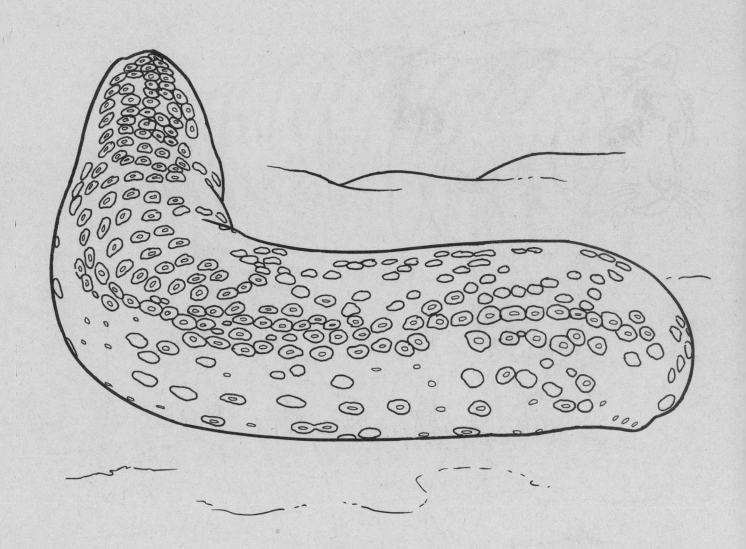

Sea Cucumber

Buffalo

Whale

MATCHING TAILS
Match the tail to the correct animal!

See Answers

Baby pandas open their eyes within 4-8 weeks after birth.

Cheetah

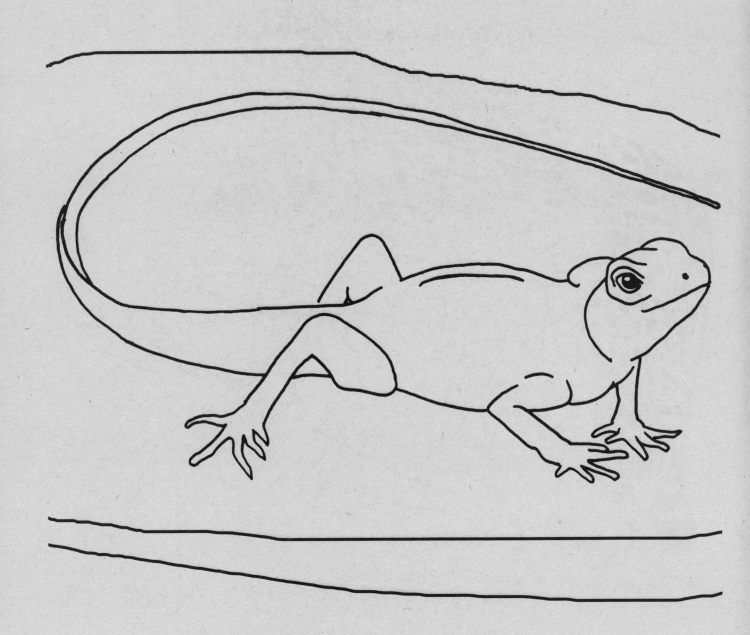

Lizard

A frog is a type of amphibian.

Killer Whale

SNAKE LIZARD TURTLE

H	F	L	C	I	T
S	F	F	N	U	M
N	E	H	R	N	P
A	R	T	X	U	S
K	L	X	S	D	L
E	E	N	V	L	K
D	R	A	Z	I	L
C	X	B	D	N	B

REPTILE SEARCH
Find and circle all of the names of these reptiles in the puzzle! Look up, down, across and diagonally.

See Answers

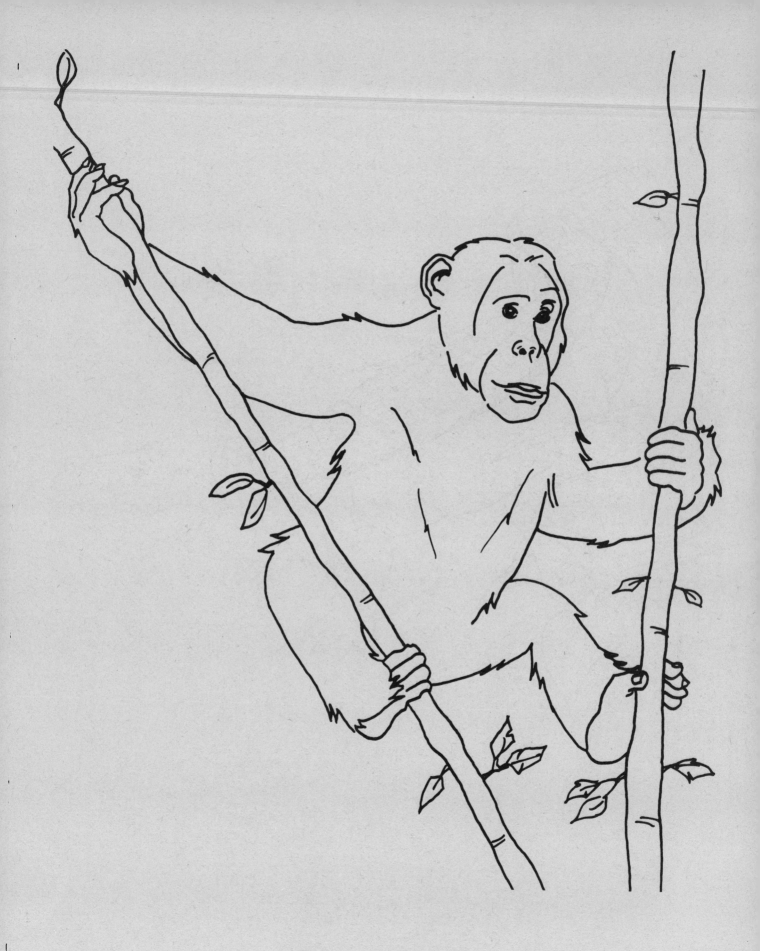

Chimpanzee

Alligator

Deer

Snake

Wild Boar

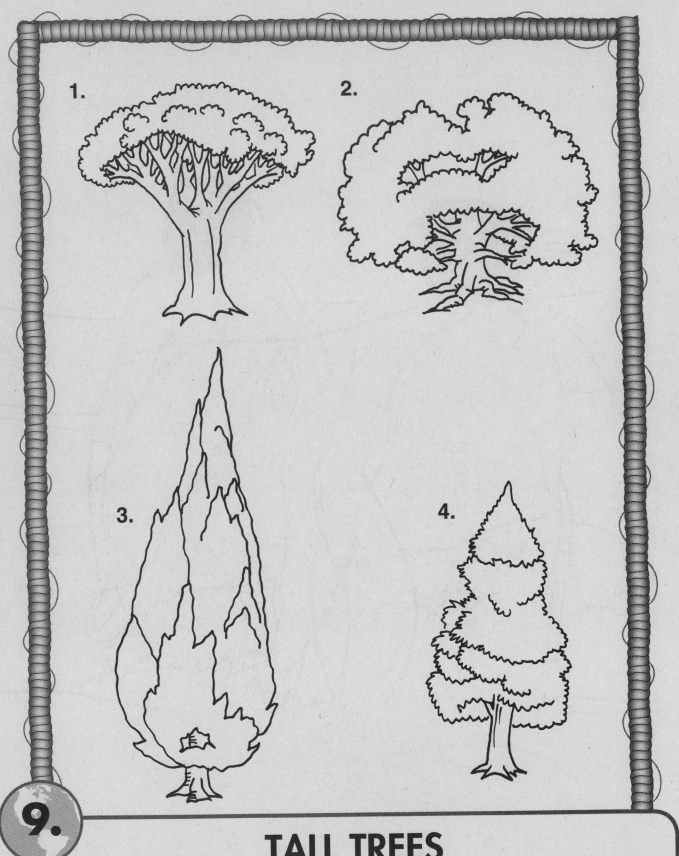

1.

2.

3.

4.

9.

TALL TREES

Trees come in all different shapes and sizes.
Circle the tree that is the tallest!

See Answers

Penguins

Peacock

Antelope

Bear Cub

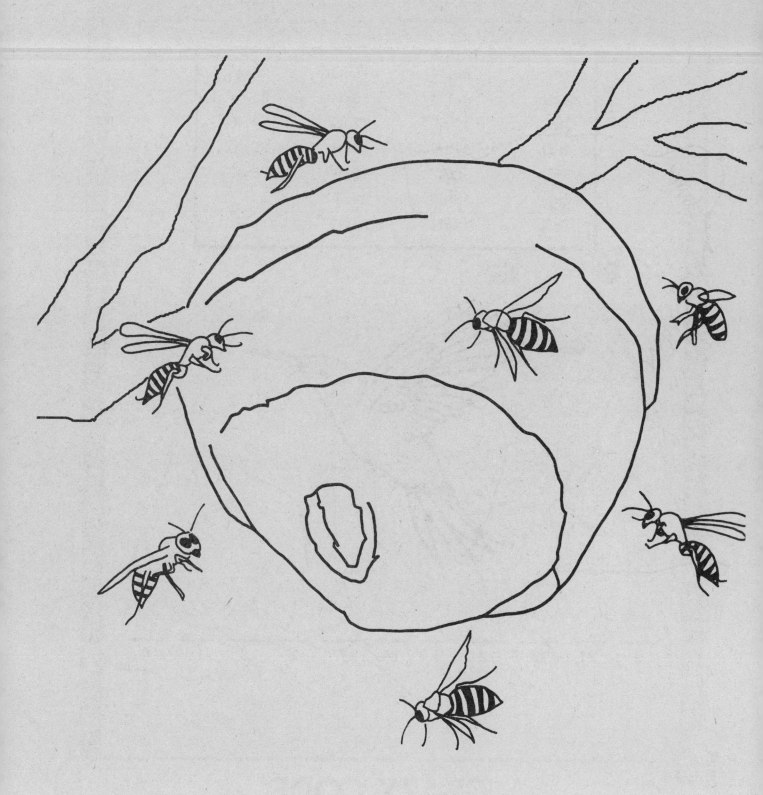

Bees

1=A	8=H	15=O	22=V
2=B	9=I	16=P	23=W
3=C	10=J	17=Q	24=X
4=D	11=K	18=R	25=Y
5=E	12=L	19=S	26=Z
6=F	13=M	20=T	
7=G	14=N	21=U	

___ ___ ___ ___ ___ ___ ___ ___ ___ ___ ___
8   21   13   13   9   14   7   2   9   18   4

10.

CRAZY CODE

Using the code, write the letters on the lines
to find out which bird is the smallest
in the world!

See Answers

Mountain Goats

**Mountains cover 24% of the
land surface on our planet.**

**The giraffe is the
tallest animal on land.**

Flamingo

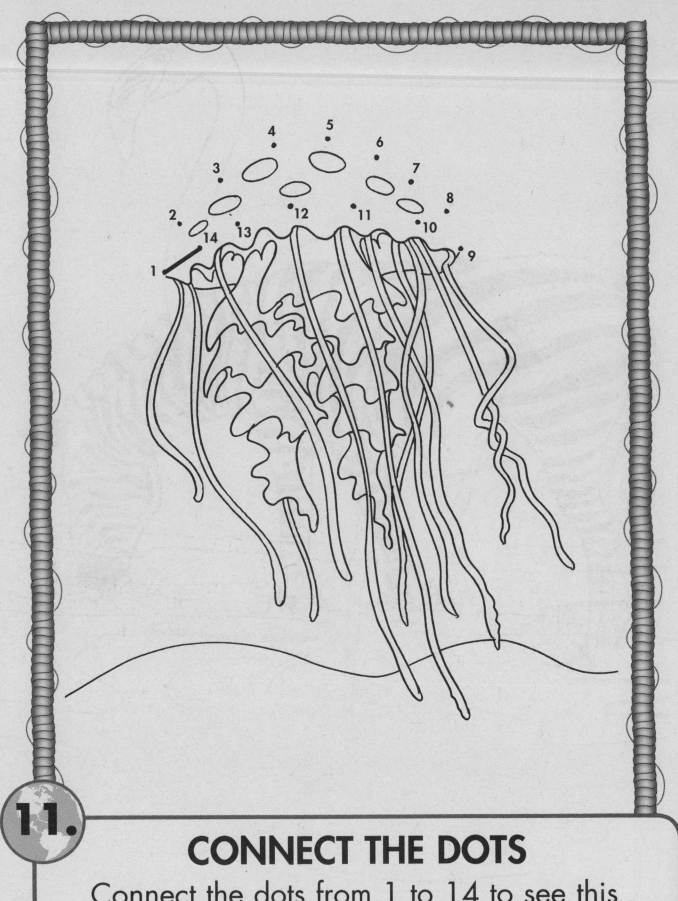

11.

CONNECT THE DOTS
Connect the dots from 1 to 14 to see this
poisonous sea creature!

See Answers

Zebra

Pythons

Dolphin

Jungles only cover 6% of the Earth's surface.

Kangaroo

A manatee is a type of mammal and is often known as the Sea Cow.

12.

A-MAZE-ING BIRDS
Help the mother bird find her babies by following the path through the maze!

See Answers

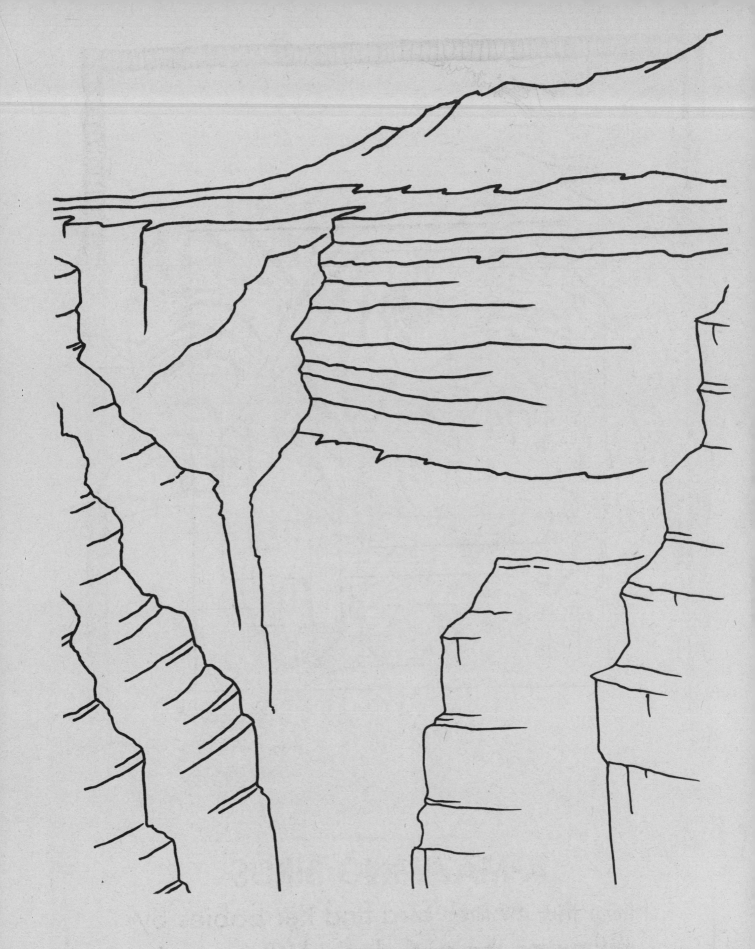

Canyon

Tiger

Raccoon

Ostrich

Lion

G A K A O O N R

_ _ _ _ _ _ _ _

AUSTRALIAN ANIMALS

Unscramble the word to find out which bouncy animal is primarily found in Australia!

See Answers

Ostrich

Jaguar

Bear

Shrimp

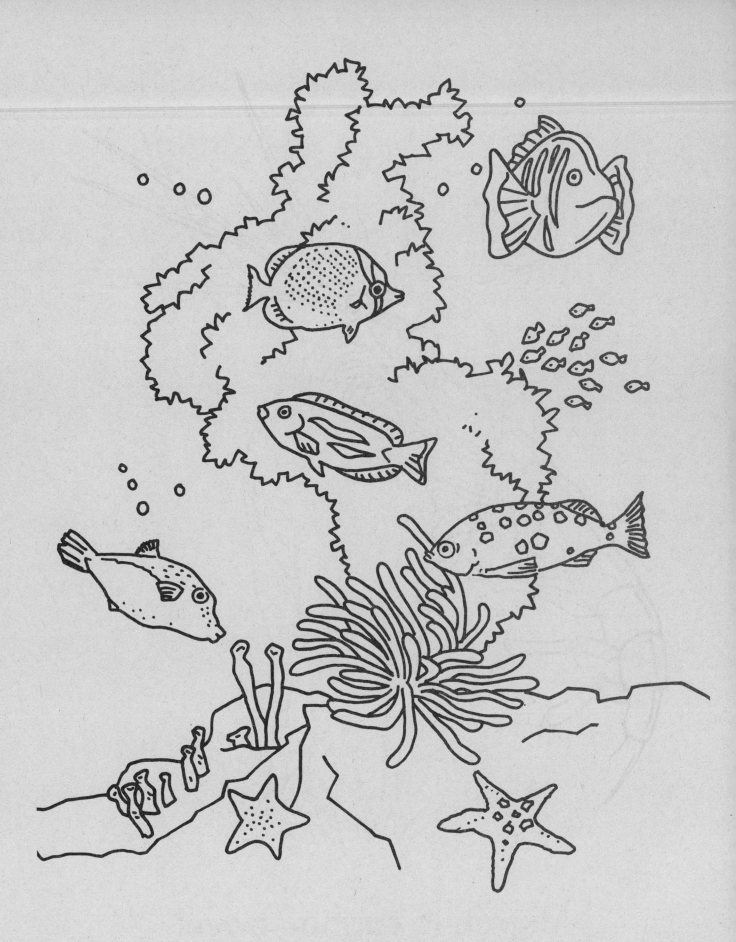

Reef

Migrating caribou travel farther than any other land animal!

All of the peaks that are over 26,000 feet are in the Himalayas.

Eagle

Lion

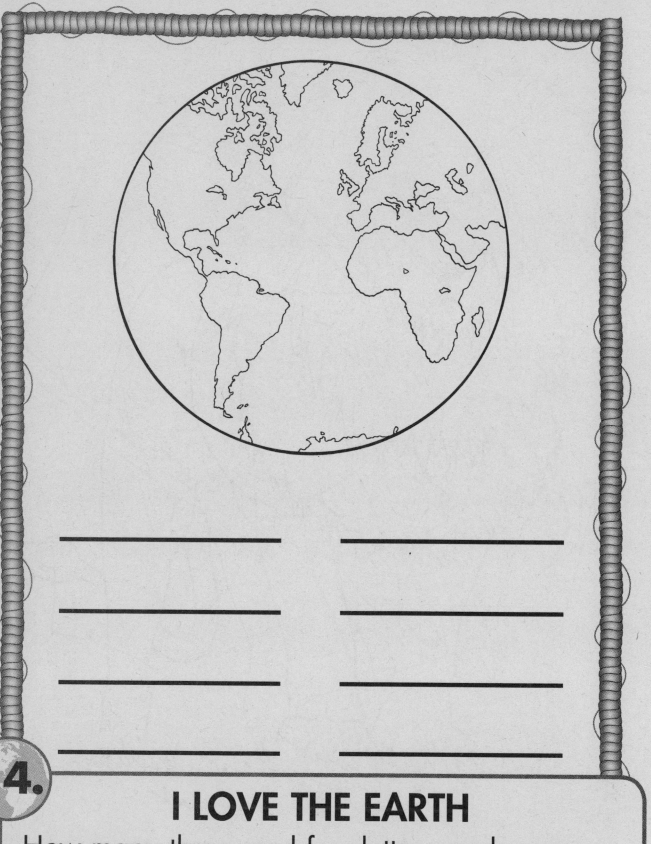

14.

I LOVE THE EARTH

How many three- and four-letter words can you make from the letters in the words I LOVE THE EARTH? Write them on the lines.

See Answers

Spider

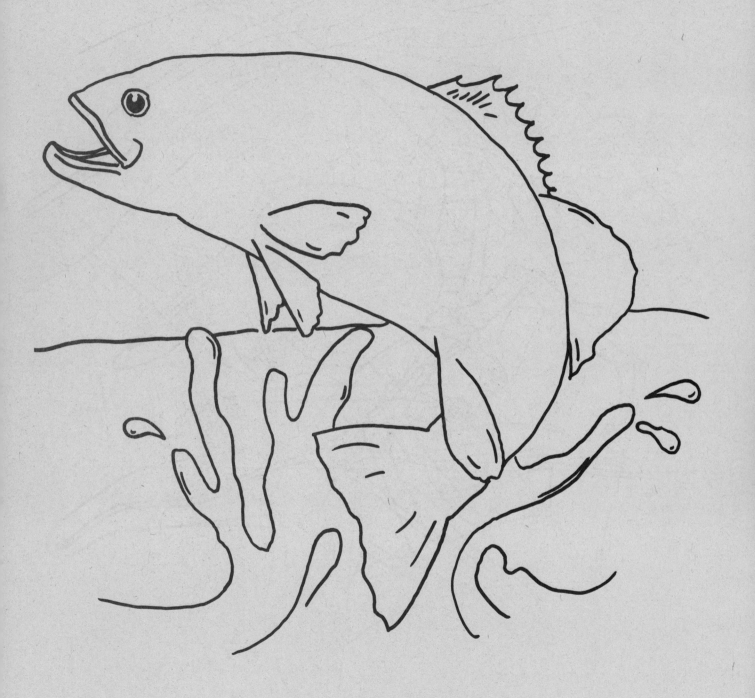

Salmon

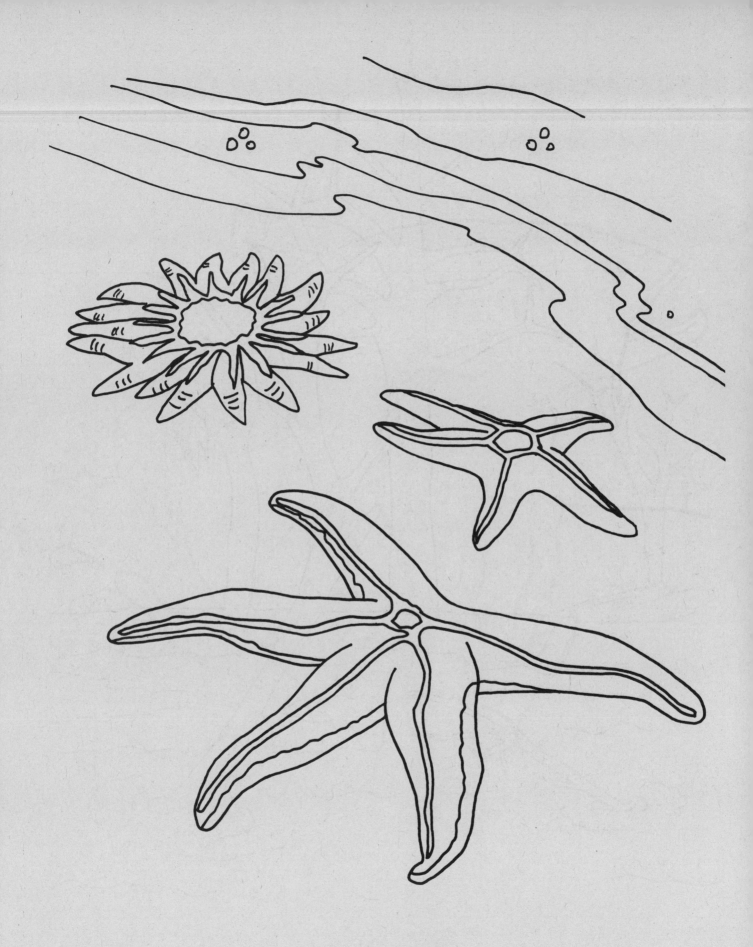

Starfish

Swamp

Elephants' ears are big so they can disperse heat and stay cool.

ANSWERS

1.

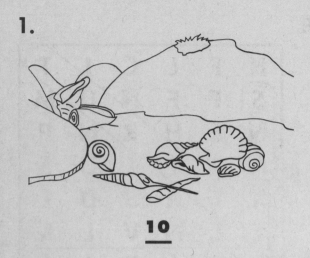

10

3.

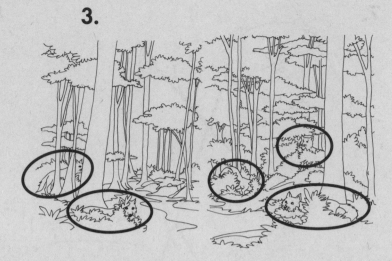

4.

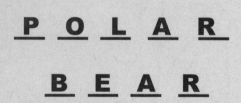

P O L A R

B E A R

5.

6.

14

ANSWERS

7.

8.

H	F	L	C	I	T
S	F	F	N	U	M
N	E	H	R	N	P
A	R	T	X	U	S
K	L	X	S	D	L
E	E	N	V	L	K
D	R	A	Z	I	L
C	X	B	D	N	B

9.

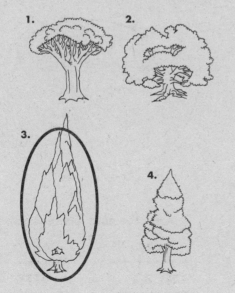

1.
2.
3.
4.

10.

<u>H</u>	<u>U</u>	<u>M</u>	<u>M</u>	<u>I</u>	<u>N</u>	<u>G</u>	<u>B</u>	<u>I</u>	<u>R</u>	<u>D</u>
8	21	13	13	9	14	7	2	9	18	4

ANSWERS

11.

12.

13.

K A N G A R O O

14.

SOME POSSIBLE ANSWERS ARE:

LOT	HAVE
HEAT	HIT
TAIL	THAT
ROLE	TIE